Jurgis Petraskas

Poems by Anthony Petrosky

JURGIS PETRASKAS

Louisiana State University Press / Baton Rouge and London

1983

Copyright © 1983 by Anthony Petrosky
Manufactured in the United States of America

Designer: Barbara Werden
Typeface: Linotron Baskerville
Typesetter: G&S Typesetters, Inc.
Printer: Thomson-Shore

The author wishes to thank the editors of the following journals in which some of these poems first appeared for their support and their permission to reprint the poems in this book: *Agni Review* ("My Father Is"), *Choice* ("Illusions"), *Cincinnati Poetry Review* ("For Luck"), *Georgia Review* ("The Other Life"), *Iowa Review* ("Change"), *Ironwood* ("Rain: The Funeral: The Woman's Voice," "Mourning Cloak," "Speaking to Myself," "Crayfish," "Return to the Woods," "A Pennsylvania Family," "Land Song at the Exeter Mines," "Photograph," and "Late Morning"), *Modern Poetry Studies* (an early version of "Late Morning"), *New Salt Creek Reader* ("Ornaments," "Widow's Poem," and "Crazy Wife"), *raccoon* ("Going Blind: The Woman's Voice" and "Jerusalem, Pittsburgh"), and *Rapport* ("V.A. Hospital").

Heatherstone Press originally published an early version of "Friday, the Day Mariana Penko Quit Cooking for Her Husband" in its *Garland Edition*. Sections of this book were also published as limited edition chapbooks by Ironwood Press (*Waiting Out the Rain*), Rook Press (*New Lives*), and Inland Boat, Porch Publications (*The Look of Things*). Individual poems were also published as broadsides by the Bellevue Press and the Slow Loris Press.

"Marcus Nathaniel Simpson: His Voice" is based on a conversation with him when he was seventy-nine years old in an incredible study of time by Thomas J. Cottle and Stephen L. Klineberg, *The Present of Things Future: Exploring of Time in Human Experience* (New York, 1974). Some of the lines in the poem are Mr. Simpson's. "Land Song at the Exeter Mines" paraphrases a line from James Wright's poem "Red Jacket's Grave."

The author also wishes to express his gratitude to the Pennsylvania Council on the Arts for a fellowship and to the MacDowell Colony for a residency fellowship which allowed him to complete this collection.

Library of Congress Cataloging in Publication Data
Petrosky, Tony.
Jurgis Petraskas:poems.

I. Title.
PS3566.E858J8   1983   811'.54   82-18003
ISBN 0-8071-1091-4 (pbk.)
ISBN 0-8071-1092-2

Winner of the Walt Whitman Award for 1982

Sponsored by the Academy of American Poets, the Walt Whitman Award is given annually to the winner of an open competition among American poets who have not yet published their first books of poetry.

Judge for 1982: Philip Levine.

*For my family
and in memory of James Wright*

All a man can be sure of is what he gets here on earth. He gets it here or he never gets it at all. Don't comfort yourself that what you have to bear with in life will be made up by felicity in heaven, or that the enemy who harms you will be fittingly punished in hell, for what you get here on earth, whether it's riches or poverty, happiness or sorrow, is all you ever get, and what you want or have merited has nothing to do with it. The pleasant days, the quiet places, the money jingling in the pocket, the cities and countries you would like to see, the things you would like to do—all this you enjoy here on earth or forever go without. There's no making up what you missed, no going back; no triumphs for the long-suffering, no fiery torments for the evildoers. Nobody keeps accounts, and once the worms have finished with them the murderer rests as peacefully as his victims.

Mike Dobrejcak in
Out of This Furnace

THOMAS BELL

Contents

1

2

1

JURGIS PETRASKAS, THE WORKERS' ANGEL, ORGANIZES THE FIRST MINERS' STRIKE IN EXETER, PENNSYLVANIA

Draped in khaki, Jurgis
who steals chickens
makes his way in the black dust
among the workers—so tired
and slow—trying to persuade them
that some abstraction is worth their jobs.
Jurgis with fireflies in his head.
       The old women sipping from a little bottle
of whiskey shake their heads and pray
to Matka Boża, virgin of virgins,
to deliver us from this affliction,
this crazy man who tells everyone
God is not good enough to them.
The girls don't sing on the steps anymore,
Matka Boża, and all we hear is the tune
Jurgis's troublesome bones play.
       When the sun reaches the highest place in the sky
everyone stops and eats while the good lord of the day
spreads his shadows over the dreams of his people—
the hot bodies in the mines, the streets
where nothing moves
until we stir like flies. Tomorrow
the angel of his own lord,
the weight of his passion, digs his own grave
inciting the miners to riot in Memorial Street
where the troopers kneel hunched over
their black Fords, tipped off, waiting.

A PENNSYLVANIA FAMILY

1.

The Petraskases used to run whiskey
along with milk deliveries
during the Depression. Cows, chickens,
ducks, and goats cluttered the small yard
until the second house was built
and hard times over.

The Wyoming Valley was never rich,
except for the mines,
taking more life
than it gave. The women
held the families together.
Scrawny, rough-handed
women who could pick mushrooms
by sight, knew the feeling
of good mash and tasted
with their fingers.

Like patches of brown moss
their children grew
to the dress factories,
farms, and mines.

2.

Night shift, small change
in the bars, the men want to sleep:
apples, pears for a second, a century
away from slag and coal.

Old man Petraskas worked the mines
until he died and refused to let his sons
do the same. They worked the stills,
delivering what finally saved them,
the whiskey.

3.

I lean hard against my brain;
slowly
like a wet sack of sugar
an old lady
in a noisy green chair
rocking back and forth
calls my name:
Antanas, Antanas.

Secretly,
like sounds
pressing against the night,
I am making my way
to join her.

GOING BLIND: THE WOMAN'S VOICE

My husband, hot, drunk,
shouts to his friends.
It's a good thing I know the streets
and market places. All morning
he chatters away, relentless as the heat.
    When I face the light
and hold my hand up,
I can barely see the shadows of tree branches
hanging low like the extended hands
of someone reaching for me in the morning sun.
Pani, my friend, helps with meals and washing.
She knows my children's faces and remembers
a strange haze like a child's watercolor—
red, yellow, and slightly blue—fills the sky
in July and that the dogs barking and running
from the hot days into the streets at night
keep me awake.
    So the journey continues
out into the heavy sun, the side of the hill
surrounded by grapevines where my mind wanders
to the sounds of men working in the fields,
my old man pretending, thinking he knows
what he doesn't, thinking
things work out for the best.

FRIDAY, THE DAY MARIANA PENKO QUIT COOKING
FOR HER HUSBAND

July:
the cats stretch under the trees' oppressive heat
as she runs out of the house cursing her husband.
He pisses away the money.
The men in t-shirts playing cards on the porch
stop talking and turn to watch.
"Busza Mariana," one of them mutters, "hold your tongue,"
but nothing surprises them.

The screen door slams,
and the day shatters.
Her flowered dress disappears in a blur.
The men light cigarettes and go back to talking politics
while the boys kick a ball in the dusty street.
No one visits the old couple anymore,
and it has been a long time since they stood in the doorway
holding each other.

JERUSALEM, PITTSBURGH

for Lynn Emanuel

Suliman Barakat, round and evasive,
says there aren't any choices. Outside
the landscape is sand. Your friend
loves his sons and the heat rising
through the lemon trees in midafternoon,
takes good care of his wife
and saves money. The wind picks up
and blows your life around without any trouble.

I couldn't imagine what besides despair
could drive you to this place. Steel mills.
Switch engines in the valley crawling
among iron sheds with the same slow motion
of memory—old houses filled with tenants
and TVs. A dull sun
in a yellow painting closes in.
You imagine alternatives,
the eloquence of green in the summer,
a need to travel, the streets
quiet at last.

STREETLIGHT: THE WEDDING PHOTOGRAPH

Shrubs along the sidewalk glisten with a light coat of rain.
The guests crowd onto a large newly painted porch to pose
for the departure. The sweet smell of postwar spring
hangs in the air. My mother and father stand out,
poised against a background of relatives.
My mother's sisters, dressed so splendidly
in taffeta and tulle gowns,
hardly look like they work in the cigar factory
along the river. My father's mother, Victoria,
a short stern woman, stares at him.
She braces herself against the stone pillar.

SLAUGHTERING CHICKENS

Dressed in an oiled leather apron, blue babushka on her head, Victoria Petraskas moves through the crooked doorways of the old house, past dilapidated tin sheds, apple and chestnut trees, to the cluttered yard where she grabs the first fat chicken to cross her path. Standing straight as she can, clutching the neck in both of her hands, she stares into the mud. Her husband returns for the day from the woods with baskets of mushrooms and a sheepshead as large as the trunk of a tree. Silent, careful not to let anyone know where he found it, he steps into the yard; twigs snap. The neck of the chicken breaks. In one graceful movement, she swings the body down on the block of pine. Holding the scrawny legs in her left hand, she lifts the axe from the ground and brings it around over her shoulder. The wind sounds like an ocean in the red pines. The axe comes down; the head falls into the basket for heads; its body convulses as the blood drains into a battered metal bucket.

PHOTOGRAPH

Through rain I see huge moonless spaces,
intricate scars in the earth,
a fine thread of water.
Two voices in the clouded space name the planets,
the moon, the earth.

Postwar mining town,
the color of stone and Kodachrome
fades into the women's eyes. They're there
in Exeter, Pennsylvania, counting, chanting in Lithuanian
the names of mines and mills with the same slow song
that seeps through the dark tunnels.

So this is the way silent things speak.
Who told the stars their names?
Certainly not the man in the photograph
too long in paper mills
where the only stars are in his swollen eyes.

There is little to be said
for that misguided winter
when my father went to work the mills.

V.A. HOSPITAL

in memory of John Makstutis

Yesterday I didn't know this place.
Today I wished you were dead.

The hallways are hollow drum logs.
This is the white history of death:
TV, cigarettes, magazines,
all the stupid charities
cluttered on a table.

I am the stranger here.
I have never seen a man alive with his face cut off
as clean as steel below his eyes.
In the name of Christ, how do you live?
Is it the gray spiders clinging
to your eyes that keep you alive?

My own guilt clings to your eyes.
In a dream, I hear the echoes of women
pounding these halls to love you.

From the outside I bring nothing of use.

12

CRAYFISH

There's more rain
than sun this summer.
The glass of the atmosphere
is dripping,
dripping.
The constant drumming
of pain in my father's wrists
feeds on this fucking weather.
He downs beers and aspirins
one after another
trying to kill the pain,
only it doesn't die.
His ankles and knees swell
as it works inward.

Like a heavy-handed blacksmith
the dampness and gray
can slam through you.
I feel the uselessness
of his wrists in mine.

My father used to be a carpenter.
Now he pushes buttons
supervising what's left.
Rain is filling underpasses.
He moves slowly;

headlights probe
for the dry blacktop.

THE KNIFE SHARPENER

The knife sharpener comes slowly, gimpily up the street ringing his tinny bell. His brown suit looks neat compared to his wild, dangling hair. The boys playing on the corner stop to follow him. They surround the grindstone when a woman in a green quilted housecoat and red slippers brings a big steel knife. He sharpens with his thumb gliding the blade across then up then across then over the stone. His hands wrinkle like the skin of hands in the sun, or snow, or wind all the time. A piece of his left thumb is missing and flat like his chin where it looks as though a knife just grazed. He doesn't say anything; the woman shuffles back to her house, and the boys go back to their corner with their hands and arms moving wildly through the air in imaginary knife fights.

MARCUS NATHANIEL SIMPSON: HIS VOICE

Everyone around me talked about death
all night long when I almost died
in a wooden shack of an army hospital.
Here the men sleep on their backs,
their cheeks and thin lips barely reveal
air passing in and out of their mouths.
Listen, there aren't many who could do what I can,
look out across the entire span of my life, any life,
and see the way it comes together—
the small secrets, disguises, an old house
with long high rooms, the silent dialogues
with myself, the gestures, my brown-haired blue-eyed
lover I'd love behind everyone's back
as the sun rises and rises in those mornings
with no place to go. Very little goes away
for good and that is a comfort to an old man
who has known loneliness.

I knew there would come a day
when I would be by myself.
It was February, cold damp color of mud
and wood, when my wife died. A day
hasn't gone by when I don't think of her.
Yes, I remember. The past gets longer.
Everything changes.
A man has got to learn that being alone

is the most important part of his life.
And sometimes when I write letters
to a few distant people, I think
we can live too long.
But I know, in the heart of all my years,
that not for a second do I believe it.

2

We walk through ourselves meeting robbers,
ghosts, giants, old men, young men, wives, widows, brothers-in-love.
But always meeting ourselves.

JAMES JOYCE

MORNING, MEADOW, WIFE

When I woke this morning, still groggy from sleep, the sun was just coming over the tops of the pines and the meadow looked like a landscape on a planet soaked in eerie light silver light. I expected to see a large graceful animal like an elk or antelope grazing on the good thick green. I remembered once, in the northern wilderness, you wanted to hold an animal as sleek as an antelope and feel the fine lines of grace and movement stretch into muscle, bone. I remembered too that when you stoop or half lie, naked, on the bed bending your legs with your head down waiting for me, you are the shape of grace and movement. When I enter, you are warm and wet. Sometimes on slow mornings like this, tucked away in the woods by myself, I think it is possible to be lost for the rest of my life in the rhythm of our bodies, your legs bent, ready to spring. It is a long dream, isn't it?

ILLUSIONS

The sky melts
down a yellow rope
of sun.
A thin line
at the end of the lake,
morning mist,
fools my mind
as a woman,
a small cloud flung into space,
moves over the water
and disappears.

The part of my mind
I misunderstand
tells me beads are magical,
and words—
turquoise, azurite,
topaz—
the stones of eloquence,
power.

The day slips on
and moves through the house.
In the distance church bells ring.
Noon. Dull and uneasy
the city floats
in its own haze.
Alone, I am myself,
anyone.

WIDOW'S POEM

in memory of Pablo Neruda, Chile, 1973

For the past three days I've watched the clock preach,
some half-mad jack-in-the-pulpit
going over and over promises of sleep.
Soldiers are sawing planks for coffins.
There are women everywhere pleading
for their sons and husbands,
and the repeating sounds of seconds and minutes
fill the yellow fields with more corpses.
The hips of my husband
turn dark as the earth—
lead, stone.
I talk to the ocean to stay alive.

A darkness reaches under my skirt
and pulls me to the earth.
Grateful for anything, I know the trees
still belong to the air, the ground, animals—
the sea to whoever reaches it first.
I am thinking about the woods
where we slept together,
how safe it was,
moist eucalyptus trees.
Never mind time; it's over.

RAIN: THE FUNERAL: THE WOMAN'S VOICE

after César Vallejo

All morning the cold rain
has banged on the door.
No one will let it in.

What am I doing here
kissing the lips of a dead man?
What is this place?

This earth dressed like a man
holds what I wanted most. Left behind
with a fire pawing my insides
I still feel the violent flower,
the other women who sipped a little of you.
Bastard. Naked,
in the middle of the night
a long length of ruby-colored rope burns
in my stomach. I wrap it around
and around my fingers, feed it anything but love.
That's all I owe. I tell my dreams
to grant wishes slowly, deliberately.
In my own good time, I will answer the rain.

WHAT KEEPS US

I have always wanted obscurity . . .

LYNN EMANUEL

There is so much sadness here.
Didn't you say it yourself,
we lost the courage to take risks.
Last night as I stood in the cove
listening to the ocean, the lights
dropped down the cliffs to the other side of the bay
where it is easy to be alone.
But you, you go into things—
a ship, a body, crazy Ann of Walsingham
throwing tarot in front of the tower
where the king's executioner waits
for your lover, then you
in this strangely sullen city
where I have wanted to be your lover.
Whatever we are or aren't,
whatever we are afraid of,
obscurity, as seductive as it is,
is not what we imagine
on nights like these
trying to redesign our lives
to see how anything after this is over
and the worms have finished with us
must be absolutely unlike what we know
or can know, and how unlike us
to believe in it.

ANGELS

for Ina Mullis

As the sun begins to set, a blond curly-haired boy
rides past in the lifeguard's bright orange Jeep.
A young black woman in a turquoise leotard
and a red hair band runs by talking
to a laughing friend. An old man in shades of red
looks like a lamp in his wide Panama hat.
He walks north with purpose.
A woman with a husky voice swings her arms,
marching south, talking to herself.
The tall palms lean inland in the almost gone light.
The ocean with its thin infinity
pulls in, powerful, monotonous.
A young girl passes in a gold and black striped shirt.
A pair of fluorescent green shorts and a red visor
heads south, again. The sun explodes
against a clear green sky over the eucalyptus
and a night heron passes through the sun as a woman
stops to tie her shoe then runs away.
Cormorants and pelicans congregate to eat fish washing in
with the tide, and to the north a long brown cloud
rises in the air, Los Angeles.
In the distance, south of Point Loma
great aircraft carriers sit on the water
and angels land on the edge of the sea
in explosions of stars and thunder.

CARL PERUSICK

Tonight I think of him, my kind unaggressive friend
who gestured to me like a man caught in the rain,
sitting on the rocks along the river.
I remember the fog glistening in the faded light
and the bewildered houses
walking into the river on their skinny wooden legs
while we hauled logs out of the water.
When I cut my foot on a piece of glass,
he carried me home on his back
and I remember, too, our reflection in the store windows
looked like a large upright turtle.
We had built a raft from driftwood
and that night we almost made it across.

MOURNING CLOAK

1.

I can walk out of this town
and back and believe
in my freedom. But everything
isn't right. Last night's
wine is still in my blood,
and there are times I walk
nowhere like a caged animal
knowing there is no way out
of any human town.
This morning my head is empty,
no sense cursing anyone;
thinking about death or love
doesn't help. When love is gone
I'll walk out to the trees
wildly waving my arms
chasing the late winter snow.

2.

Beyond the break in trees
the Penn Central still hauls
coal and the soft mumblings
of an old man
trying to get some sleep.
Next to me, my wife
doesn't hear the train

and the bewildered language
of my dream leaves me staring
at a bright ball of light
barreling its way from Meshoppen
to Wilkes-Barre. Last night blurs
somewhere in the back of my head.
I want warmth this morning.
A few minutes ago I was asleep
not worrying about myself or this house.
Now I want to stay in bed
until I get rid of this goddamn headache.

3.

These hands on my eyes easing out the light
are my wife's. Velvet brown yellow laced wings
whose name I barely remember.
     Mourning cloak
butterfly stopped on a long vine near the window
to watch me wake.
My grandfather, the old man
who built this house,
loved the strange English names;
mourning cloak,
she's the one I love best.

ORNAMENTS

Leather,
tough dried skin of animals
soft from use. Your feet
quiet as the hide protecting them.
I begin with praise
for the animals.

The deer graze along the tree line
where instinct tells them it's safer.

Two perfectly round eyes
have been following me all night.
From the porch to the stream
to the shitter and back to the cabin.

Gold,
two bright circles mimic the sun.
Earrings.
My eyes are surprised.
Even the shadows are filled with heat
in this room. Your skin
wet as the humid summer air.

Flax, cotton,
a dress made of cotton
dyed red.
This is a fine dress;
it folds easily
over a chair.

I stare red-faced,
the boy who loves your breasts.

IN PRAISE OF HANDS

Rain, thunder, and lightning drop against the city. Gray and black clouds move at tremendous speeds to the ocean miles downriver where the land parts into a bay like a hand whose fingers hold on with a tentative grip and stretch out along the coast—complicated, bony.

My grandmother could hold an apple so her fingers bent and curved around the sloping skin. She made peaches burst in her hands when she bit into them, and her hands, wrinkled and fragile, looked like wax when she died.

Grief leaves the hands of my mother flat, lifeless, and my father, arthritic, grimaces as his swollen hands try to twist the cap off a bottle. My son learns to use his plump almost shapeless hands in gestures I begin to recognize as his.

Hands do what we tell them to. I have watched them twisting rings, resting pensive or forlorn one on top of the other—mine sliding to your breasts and yours in the flat of my stomach and down until we move with each other in the larger hands of hips.

CRAZY WIFE

It's the third time this week
you've decided the sky's filled
with bright yellow bears
dancing
like a thousand candles,

that you drink stars
instead of water.

Are there stars in water
or water in stars?

I don't know.
But I can tell you
when I am between your legs
I dream I'm a bear
with a thousand candles
in my belly.

Look, I'm a bear!

Like you say,
when they come to get me,
they come to get you.

RESILIENCE

Tired, unable to sleep, the young woman stretches forward from the chair to straighten the black-and-white photograph of a clown laughing hysterically. The small sailboat in the stained glass window floats on dimly moonlit blues and whites of impossible departure.

She sits back, closes her eyes, and the room empties into thoughts of friends no longer friends, old lovers too far inside themselves, the few new ones noncommittal and distant. Lights from the expressway far below the house form a chain of constant twilight movement through the night.

A swatch of dull gold crosses the empty landscape as the horizon begins to glow: white walls, a field of snow, the tenuous rope of fog stretching across the lives that collapse like the sides of boxes, one at a time, two or three, year after year, imperceptible as morning.

SPEAKING TO MYSELF

I'm not living to die,
or so I tell myself.
Like the snail in the spiral cave
of a shell, I'm living for something
inside of me. My body
inside and out.
The white belly of an egg-filled trout
stares down at me from the wall
across from the ladies' john
at Bitterman's Bar.
That's the life,
out in the open woods
fishing or just taking it easy
along the beach.
Somewhere someone
fishes for a living.

The moon is very high
like the sun and earth
casting spells.
A riddle? No.
A gift:
old shells from last summer
when we needed to bring back
something beautiful—
there on the shelf

above the other junk we hauled home
smooth as the mute mixtures
of gray-blue, white,
and salt.

My wife hands me a beer
saying, "you're still here
with me," and then she brings back
summer solid as her thigh.
The one prize,
the shell inside the shell.

Curvilinear,
the space in the spiral
shell of a fat snail
is curvilinear.
I love music and this woman.
I know what I need.

$$\underline{3}$$

LISTENING TO MY SON'S HEART

It's a game we play.
Well, as much a game as I can play with a one-year-old.
It goes like this.
When I come home from work,
he's there, toddling around the kitchen, wide-eyed
in his baby blue sleeping suit
with the padded feet.
When he sees me, he smiles, and I do too,
and I imagine the sound, the *thud thud thud*
of his tiny heart that I remember
from the last time we played our game.
I stoop down so my haunches almost touch the floor
and open my arms for a hug. He walks over
in his confident but uneasy way
and we are eye to eye when he breaks into laughter,
wraps his arms around my neck, and gently
nibbles on my shoulder. I do the same,
and it's then that I hear it, his heart
much faster than mine. After a minute or so
he turns around and walks out of my arms
only to turn around again and walk back,
laughing, anticipating the hug
and, I think, the repetition. And again
I hear his heart, and again, momentarily,
an uncanny mixture of joy and fear,
happiness and anxiety overtakes me.

It is, I know, my pleasure in his life,
in his being here with us, and my fear
for him, for the difficulties yet to come.
But it is, also, a kind of self-pity;
the comfort of remorse that comes from imagining pain
juxtaposed against happiness, the permutations
of the future against the immediacy of the present,
the sound of his heart against the absence of it.

TODAY AND TOMORROW

The man across the street hammers nails into his house. I just finished cleaning my brushes, and my feet hurt from standing on the ladder all day. The sun sets in an ooze of blues and reds against the houses. Pretty soon my son goes to sleep. Today, the people who own the lot filled with garbage and overrun with weeds came and cleaned it up in the sweltering air. When I went into the city, the grocery stores were packed with people buying everything they could get their hands on, and there were long lines of cars at the gas pumps. The crazy man played his flute while I sat on the corner watching the lines wiggle like snakes as the heat rose in waves off the blacktop. My country turns on itself. There's nothing I can do. Tomorrow, I am going to wash the porch. Last night I dreamt I was digging a grave that kept filling with water, and the water was my sadness.

MACKEY

John Makstutis,
my good uncle,
lost half of the right side of his face
in Korea. A 50-calibre shell
ricocheted off a boulder into the back of his head
and out the front.

I like to think of him walking down Schooley Street
past the railroad tracks to where the road
takes off into the hills.
He was a tall man with broad shoulders
slightly bent to his right.
I see him sitting in the chair by the lamp
with the shade shaped like a cornet.
His hair is thin and dark
and hangs in a curl on his forehead.

LIBERTY AVENUE

It's so hot tonight.
The boys prowling the streets
with their shirts off,
and their girls wandering aimlessly
always seem to find someone they know
on every corner. The bars are still open too,
and the smell of fried fish hangs in the humid air.
This is the kind of night I will remember Pittsburgh for—
the kids in doorways listening to radios and smoking dope,
the blond mopsticks lined-up
in the hardware store windows
like assembly line workers,
like my father, with his silver hair
and ingratiating fatalism.

MY FATHER IS

My father is a small man
who wears flannel shirts,
silver-blue workpants,
a matching blue billed hat,
and works on an assembly line
in a shed that stretches for acres.
All day he stands on concrete,
the noise from the machines
vibrating through him.

Years ago when my sister left,
my mother lost hold of herself.
Now she wants to leave
and my father, brooding,
won't let anyone near him.

I still do not understand.
The house closes in.
I ask about my sister,
we are strangers. My mother
cooks a big meal and we eat,
talking about the neighbors and relatives,
while my father argues with the past.

ONCE WHEN I WAS WALKING UP THE STAIRS

Once, years ago, when I was walking up the stairs
to go to sleep in my grandmother's house,
I saw Aunt Darya's silver reflection
in her vanity mirror.
She was as bald as an old man.
From then on, I worried about embarrassing her
and tried not to look at her hair
or say anything about hair when she was around.
I don't think it worked,
although she never let on, except once
when we were walking behind the cabin near the river.
The air was close and filled with mosquitoes.
We had just stepped over a dead black snake
stretched across the road, shining in the moonlight,
when she slid her hand under her hair
like it was a hat, and scratched
as a half-concealed dread rose from the bottom of my heart.

LATE MORNING

The old man on the street stares past the boys
playing ball as he hurries then stops
when his wife appears at the top of the stairs
in her housecoat and slippers to tell him
he's forgotten something.

The movements stop for hours, it seems,
and warm air from the valley brings back a time
and a country where fruit trees and vineyards
fill the air with a sweetness,
when nothing matters as much
as a dark-haired girl—
so alive,
and the coolness slipping into the day.

As a small boy, he sits and watches the girls
gathering to talk to and tease everyone they run into.
Today in his memory, running away, he comes home
to find his mother dressing a boy.
His hand encloses a sun-warmed stone
and the smell of grapes fills the room.

RETURN TO THE WOODS

What's here won't welcome us.

Weird glass spiders in the pines
nod in their webs.

Clouds move in over the lake.
Winter.
A dull gray bellmetal
rings in the air.
The light breaks
in gestures of ice.

Centuries of wood:
American elm, ash, and maple
crack in the breeze.
Who feels the cold
more than the trees?

I taste the ice
and feel the forest floor.
We pick this unlikely place
to taste each other. Damp
cold leaves rub against my ass.
Another day grows thin on time;
everything we love is made of it.

TALKING WITH MY WIFE

All week the weather is bad.
Large snow clouds
pull the sky
down over our lives
and ice up the roads.

We talk
about the bones of roads
falling dead at night,
and why we are afraid of dying.

By the slight curve of the planet
a wind passes
scattering snow.

FRAGMENTS

Snow comes up between the wheels of cars and fills the street with white dust. A boy walks by packing a snowball in his bare hands; a man in a lime-colored hat leans into the blowing snow, and birds move from chimney to chimney stopping to pick at trash in the street. A crow flies across the field where I hunted crows with my father.

Across the street, a woman runs her hands over the lace drapes on the windows. Gangly iced trees crack in the front of the house—the elegance of unintention.

I remember my father rowing the old wooden boat into the channel. As I swim alongside in the mirror of water, his eyes fade. And as he rows so calmly and steadily from one shore to the other, I shut the day out and think only of him, like a boy oblivious to everything but his dreams and the tiny disassembled motor in his pocket.

CHANGE

I love to sit here
looking out this big window
in this big house at the slow, steady rain.
If I could, I would be like the light
on days like this. I would be a slow iridescent glow
rising steadily against the rain. My friends
would emerge from their houses to check the weather.
They would look up and down the street like Mrs. Stapsky
who seems to be looking for her dead husband, Heime,
every morning, and then the rain would send them back
inside their warm houses to listen to music,
but they would hesitate and look up into the sky
at the bright disc behind the white clouds,
and I would tell them to go ahead and drink their coffee
and read the papers filled with stories of violence
because even though there will be no sun today,
it is still the same as yesterday or the day before
when they sat on their porches like tourists on cruise ships
drinking beer and dreaming of people in the past
because, like me, they change by intensification or diminish.

THE OTHER LIFE

1.

It was past midnight when I looked up into the dim light
of the old man's face.
He got up to walk to the jukebox
and when he finally pulled himself back,
shaking,
a woman sang
about believing in love
and sweet time
soaked through everything.

I stood at the end of the bar,
lost for a long time
in the huge photograph
of the old city,
Pittsburgh,
Jesus.

My father worked the mills
in dingy towns like this
while my mother grew sad
in the gray days.
They could have lived here.

When I finally stepped into the cold night,
the air stood still
in a soaking rain
blocked off on either side
by swatches of buildings, warehouses.

Frank Campbell worked in a warehouse in my town
until somebody found him in the alley
with a knife in his gut.
He could have lived here, too,
with his one silent son.

3.

As for me,
I had forgotten the other life
where the dead keep their shoes,
the way grief leaks through
the roofs, the rain, the bones.

LAND SONG AT THE EXETER MINES

1.

Listen.
Along the river's east bank
an old turtle takes it easy
in fat, round mist.
Afraid of me, her children
slip into the water
where flat stones protect them.

Scrub birch, Scotch pine,
this is my grandfather's land.
He loved the slight,
fragile trees.
Drunken miner
killed a cop.
So what.
He paid for it.

2.

Dusk,
the old turtle moves
in light left behind.
I stop,
light a small fire
and listen to the sounds of animals.
The trees say acorns, apples.

55

Soft inner ears of animals
hold the melancholy songs of DPs.

3.

This earth is a door.
I want to know
who hugged these huge stones
into the ground
I wake on.
Beneath my feet everything is green and brown.

Morning.
Damn this light.

THE FIRST DAY OF SPRING AT THE CABIN
AND I STEP INTO A POOL OF LIGHT

This small cabin imbedded in silence and a colorless swatch
of bare trees is so close to what I miss in my insane business,
my ambition and money.
It reminds me of the house my grandmother loved,
always damp and warm from the coal stove,
and the irreducible security she gave it.
People think I come here to get away;
whoever wants to can believe that.
I come here to think of the people I love
in the intimacy of this peculiar light
that illuminates shades of gray and green
on the bare trees that I love
for their isolation
and definitions of curve and contour.

FOR LUCK

These pines have their own way
in the day's early heat. Still,
not an animal moving.

What matters
comes down to names,
our home, this tiny planet
going nowhere we can understand
in plenty of time.

A wind picks up,
see what there is to be seen,
push your luck, rest.

About the Author

Anthony Petrosky was born in Exeter, Pennsylvania, a small town in the northeastern part of the state. His parents are first-generation Americans. Their parents were Lithuanian immigrants. Petrosky's childhood was spent between farms and coal towns. After a time in the army, he attended graduate school at the State University of New York at Buffalo, where he studied with John Logan, earned his doctorate, and now teaches language development in the School of Education at the University of Pittsburgh. He and his wife, Patricia, have edited the Slow Loris Press (a small poetry and fiction publishing house) since 1971. They have two children, Matthew and Benjamin.